MONSTER ACROSTICS

Monster Mash

Edited By Andy Porter

First published in Great Britain in 2024 by:

Young Writers
Remus House
Coltsfoot Drive
Peterborough
PE2 9BF
Telephone: 01733 890066
Website: www.youngwriters.co.uk

Book Design by Ashley Janson

Softback ISBN 978-1-83565-725-6
Printed and bound in the UK by BookPrintingUK
Website: www.bookprintinguk.com
YB0604T

Foreword

Welcome Reader,

For Young Writers' latest competition Monster Acrostics, we asked primary school pupils to create a monster then write an acrostic poem about it. The acrostic is a fantastic introduction to poetry writing as it comes with a built-in structure, allowing children to focus on their creativity and vocabulary choice.

We live and breathe creativity here at Young Writers and we want to pass our love of the written word onto the next generation – what better way to do that than to celebrate their writing by publishing it in a book!

Featuring all kinds of crazy creatures, strange beasts and mythical monsters, this anthology is brimming with imagination and creativity, showcasing the blossoming writing skills of these young poets. They have brought their creations to life using the power of words, resulting in some brilliant and fun acrostic poems!

Each awesome little poet in this book should be super proud of themselves! We hope you will delight in these poems as much as we have.

Contents

Shocklach Oviatt CE Primary School, Malpas

Aurelia Sowerby (7) 59
Ottilia Chantler (7) 60
Esme MacNaughton (7) 61
Dulcie Wood (7) 62
Molly Jones (7) 63
Scarlet Burnett (7) 64
Ettolie-Mae Hennigan (7) 65
Beth Goggins (7) 66

St Nicholas C of E Primary School, Kenilworth

Bobby Hine (7) 67
Seren Thomas (7) 68
Orlagh Dolan (7) 70
Oliver Williams (7) 71
Henry Lough (7) 72
Him Him Leung (7) 73
Arianna De Maine (7) 74
Flora Taylor (6) 75
Emilia Tsang (7) 76
Poppy Webb (7) 77
Emil Everitt (7) 78
Jackson Proctor (7) 79
Elwood Robinson (7) 80
Bay Bell (7) 81
Lucy Wake (7) 82
Rex Griffiths (6) 83
Edie Watson (7) 84
Jaxon Kenney (7) 85
Ophelia Langley (7) 86
Pippa de Freston-Jones (7) 87
Federica Liguori (7) 88
Oscar Woodward (7) 89
Willow Beard (7) 90
Alfie Winter (7) 91
Noah Ball (6) 92
James Bury (6) 93
Noah Davies (7) 94
Joseph Bevan (7) 95
Georgia Harris (7) 96
Eva Galliana (7) 97
Olivia Miles (7) 98
Amélie Wooldridge (7) 99
Marshall Symon (7) 100
Eloisa Docker (6) 101
Kimberly Kaleta (7) 102
Henry Bentley (6) 103
Emma Ashworth (7) 104
Molly Gilbert (6) 105
Archie Rose (6) 106
Harry Slade (6) 107
William Sale (6) 108
Eliza O'Halloran (7) 109
Alexander Ruffle (7) 110
Caiden Baker (6) 111
Odysseas Karapapas-Fiamegkos (6) 112
Peppy Kay (7) 113
George (6) 114
Aria Wright (7) 115
Cobi Rowley (7) 116
Theo Thomas (7) 117

St Peter's CE Primary School, Chorley

Goodness Oyeleye (5) 118
Emily Chetwynd (5) 119
Lila Stoneman (5) 120
Fred Kilpatrick-Ivers (5) 121
William Robert McGurk (7) 122
Eliza Sharples (6) 123
Chloe Yung (6) 124
Olivia Hutchinson (7) 125
Archie Edwards (6) 126
Grace Birnie (7) 127
Leo Campkin (5) 128
Maya Kogut (4) 129
Himanya Hrulthasan (7) 130
Rupert Green (6) 131
Oroolorun Olayiwola (5) 132

Truro School Prep, Highertown

Everly Harrison (6) 133
Atticus Ducker-Cobb (5) 134
Otis Barclay (5) 135
Eleanor Viqueira (5) 136
Will Gardner (6) 137
Hugo Cudworth (5) 138
Pippa Vernon (5) 139
Arabella Coninck Farr (6) 140
Edith Hougham (6) 141
Theo Ryan (6) 142
Bethany Day (6) 143
Ernie Alken (6) 144
Albee King (5) 145
Theo Hendy (5) 146
Henry Richards (5) 147
Evie Simpson (5) 148
Clemmie Chrusciak (6) 149
William Christie (6) 150
Althea Welch (6) 151
Catherine Lambert (6) 152
Austin Pietroni (6) 153
Ted Long (5) 154

Westerton Primary Academy, Tingley

Freddie Press (5) 155
Bobby Rigby (6) 156
Oliver Green (6) 157
Emily Wilson (6) 158
Jaxon Watts (5) 159
Avah Barstow (5) 160
Maddie Bishop-West (6) 161
Dylan Lister (6) 162
Alicia Raud (5) 163
Mason Dalby (5) 164
Henry Lumley (6) 165
Dominic Pilkington (6) 166
Sophie Hedderick (5) 167
Jude Greenwood (5) 168
Grace Overend (5) 169
Eleonora Boeva (6) 170
Amelie Roadnight (6) 171
Sebastian Plauborg Varley (6) 172
Sonny Trenam-Yates (6) 173
Irhaa Khan (6) 174
Isobel Gloria Bowker (5) 175
Mila-Maria Rimkeviciute (6) 176
Orla Norton (6) 177
Sophie O'Donnell (5) 178
Lauren Maloney (6) 179
Aaron Wilson 180
Agnes Skitt (5) 181
Mia Phull (6) 182
Pearl Jamu (6) 183
Lori Wright (6) 184
Jackson Preston (5) 185
Ellie Sampson (6) 186
Ernie Morley (6) 187

The Poems

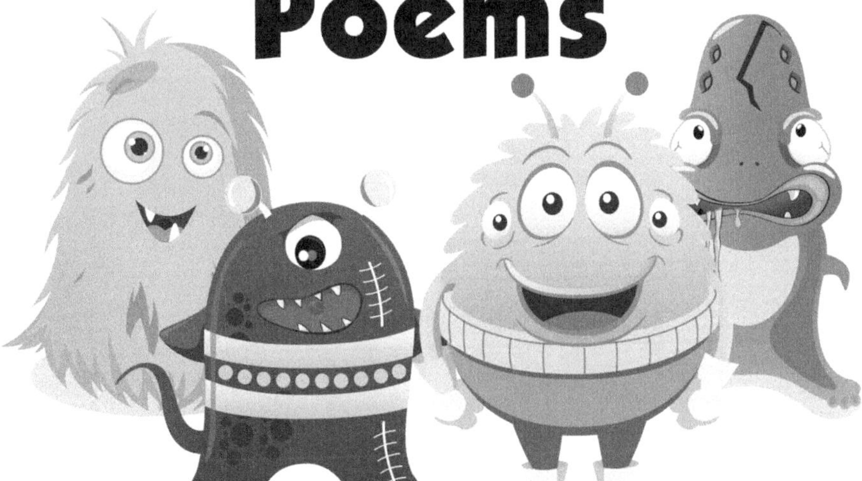

Bob The Blob

B ig and green
O n a skateboard all the time
B ob the monster is having fun.

T his monster is slimy
H e smells like wet broccoli
E ating all the food.

B ouncing around like jelly
L ook at all his googly eyes
O ld but cool
B ob the Blob is camouflaged with the grass.

Ella Thripp (7)
Highbury Primary School, Cosham

Tickles The Monster

T ickles the monster.
I can only see him.
C uddles he loves to give.
K icks me in the bum.
L oves to have fun.
E yes? He only has one.
S ecret friend of mine.

Gabrielle Barrett (7)
Highbury Primary School, Cosham

Madison

M ean monster
A ngry monster
D rinking blood monster
I t might eat me
S hould we stay?
O ften being slow
N eeds a clean.

Arin Chudley (6)
Highbury Primary School, Cosham

Bright

B right the monster
R eally likes to sing
I ntelligent and kind
G ooey skin
H appy
T hree eyes.

Alfie Cassey (7)
Highbury Primary School, Cosham

Floop

F loop is fun.
L ong tail.
O ne long trunk.
O bsessed with pizza.
P oops a lot.

Isabella Hugh (7)
Highbury Primary School, Cosham

Barry

B ad guy Barry
A lways angry
R eally hungry
R eady to eat people
Y ells a lot.

Eddie Ormston (7)
Highbury Primary School, Cosham

Nightmare Catnap

N aughty and tiny
I t has mouths on its eyeballs
G orgeous teeth, no mouth whatsoever
H ead, head, argh... no head!
T iny monstrosity
M agnificent eyes
A stun gun for one arm and a knife for the other one
R ages at everyone
E ggs are disgusting for Nightmare Catnap.

C ats are the army
A long hunt
T oo small, you can't see him
N o dogs allowed
A bloody heart
P ie is not a food for Nightmare Catnap, it's a prank.

Matthew Starling (7)
Lydlynch Infant School, Totton

Monster

M onsters love cookies, they have cookies
and booger sandwiches all day long.
O n Friday for a treat, the monsters have a
party at Monster Town.
N aughty little monsters making mischief
all day long.
S ticky, slimy monsters sticking to
everything, people try to wash them but
they don't listen.
T wo cheeky monsters snuck in my
wardrobe so beware they don't scare
you.
E vil little monster running around, nothing
stops them whatsoever.
R oaming around, you might see some
monsters drinking some tea.

Olivia Dickinson (7)
Lydlynch Infant School, Totton

Stany Long Army

S melly
T he beast likes people
A nd it is really dumb
N early has 100 arms
Y ummy people.

L ong, long arms
O n its head, it has a helicopter
N o other is smaller
G iant legs are so long.

A rmy of monsters
R eally fast
M y monster likes hot dogs
Y ucky cats.

Stanley Field (6)
Lydlynch Infant School, Totton

Monster

M onsters are scary.
O n a scary night, monsters are looking for food.
N ice monsters can be people's pets.
S ticky monsters need a bath.
T he monsters like to have a party.
E ven monsters have a party and have yummy treats.
R eally some monsters are nice and some are bad.

Pippa Wearn (7)
Lydlynch Infant School, Totton

Sivy Slime

S ometimes eats eggs
I have three eyes
V enomous fangs
Y ellow eye and pink eyes.

S illy monsters
L ikes eating chicken
I have freckles
M onsters are funny
E very day they don't have a bath.

Ryker Whitcher (7)
Lydlynch Infant School, Totton

Goobaloo

G oing on a ride-along.
O n the corridors, they run.
O n the roof, they jump.
B iting people on the leg.
A very little blob of slime.
L eaping everywhere.
O n the scary day.
O ff they go on a holiday, yippy!

Elena Duma (7)
Lydlynch Infant School, Totton

Monster

M onsters are very hairy
O range monsters run down the streets
N ice monsters
S cary monsters scare people
T he monsters like food
E ats bugs
R iding on each other's backs.

Amelia Smith (6)
Lydlynch Infant School, Totton

Gigantic

G reen toenails
I t eats flies
G rabs leaves all the time
A cts like an ant
N aughty like a black panther
T ongue is very long
I s greedy
C old like ice cream.

Olive Scott (5)
Lydlynch Infant School, Totton

Monster

M onsters have blue fur.
O nly fifty centimetres.
N eeds to eat meat.
S inging monsters sing.
T he jelly they make is green.
E yes are green.
R un, and don't stop.

Charlie Rogers (7)
Lydlynch Infant School, Totton

Bonkers

B reathes
O nly nocturnal
N ever does what it's told
K ind monster
E ats vegetables
R ummages through everything
S illy and creepy.

Miles Corbett (5)
Lydlynch Infant School, Totton

Catnap

C an eat children.
A lways angry.
T hey all have long tongues.
N ow they're all naughty.
A lways they're awesome.
P lays with purple peas.

Reuben Scott (7)
Lydlynch Infant School, Totton

Hairy

H as sharp, pointy claws.
A lways likes to eat juicy fruits.
I have orange, fluffy hair.
R un away, monsters are coming.
Y ucky, slimy, colourful monsters.

Nieve Burton (7)
Lydlynch Infant School, Totton

Smelly

S limy monsters.
M onsters are naughty.
E veryone hates monsters.
L ikes to eat people.
L ikes to take people.
Y ucky little monsters.

William Bridges (7)
Lydlynch Infant School, Totton

Gigantic

G reen hair
I s cool
G rabs a burger
A ngry monster
N ice and friendly
T ries to run
I t is fluffy
C old nose.

Harry Marks (6)
Lydlynch Infant School, Totton

Spikey

S illy when I leave
P ink, blue and red
I t is very naughty
K ind never
E very day he likes roaring
Y ou are my monster.

Grace Ghide-McRae (7)
Lydlynch Infant School, Totton

Smelly

S melly monsters.
M onsters are scary.
E ating bugs.
L ying monsters.
L ikes smelly things.
Y ou cannot trust them!

Tilly Rogers (6)
Lydlynch Infant School, Totton

Rainbow

R ainbow
A friendly monster
I t can bite
N ice monster
B eing friendly
O n a rock
W et from swimming.

Dante Delegate (6)
Lydlynch Infant School, Totton

Scary

S ome monsters have three legs.
C ome to the monster lab.
A monster can bite really hard.
R eally scary.
Y ou better run.

Elijah Noice (7)
Lydlynch Infant School, Totton

Blobby!

B lack and blue eyes
L oves food
O nly likes spots
B egging for treats
B eing an animal
Y anking shoes around.

Fletcher Green (6)
Lydlynch Infant School, Totton

Fluffy

F luffy blue fur
L ovely cute monster
U gly teeth
F ussy tummy
F unny laughs
Y ummy chocolate fingers.

Lyarna Appleton (6)
Lydlynch Infant School, Totton

Curly

C urly red fur like lava
U nusual green laser eyes
R ainy teeth
L ovely, happy monster
Y ummy and precious.

Brooklyn Cull (6)
Lydlynch Infant School, Totton

Clubs

C omes out at night.
L oves smelly things.
U nder the bright stars.
B umpy rock monsters.
S tinky monster.

Bethany Gain (5)
Lydlynch Infant School, Totton

Speedy

S limy monster
P lanting flowers
E gg and more
E veryone laughs
D one day
Y ummy, yummy, yum.

Oscar Allwood (6)
Lydlynch Infant School, Totton

Gooey

G rabs food
O nly eats pizza
O ften sleeps in a cave
E ats chicken all day
Y ucky, smelly feet.

AJ Bewley-Crespin (6)
Lydlynch Infant School, Totton

Fluffy

F luffy and cute
L ovely and kind
U gly but nice
F unny and cool
F ussy
Y ummy.

Sofia Garrett (6)
Lydlynch Infant School, Totton

Pink

P ink is the only colour he is.
I maginative.
N ever does what he's told.
K ind and helpful.

Robbie Radford (6)
Lydlynch Infant School, Totton

Fluffy

F luffy
L ovely
U seful
F riendly
F unny
Y ellow eyes.

Hugo Johnson (6)
Lydlynch Infant School, Totton

Infinity Bob

I nfinity Bob is
N ice and healthy,
F un and a wish granter.
I f they are
N ice and healthy and fun,
I nfinity Bob will grant a wish for them.
T hen they will be happy and like,
"Y ay!" and then they will...

B e so happy with their wish.
O ne wanted to go on a cloud to
B e happy for their nice, wonderful wish.

Sophia Iacovides (6)
Oakthorpe Primary School, Palmers Green

Enormous Lizard!

M ean and monstrous
I s always scary
N eeds darkness to glow blue
U gly like a dragon
S lides on his tail.

O ften eats everything
N ever sleeps
E yes as black as night.

Theron (7)
Oakthorpe Primary School, Palmers Green

Tough As Stone!

T errified of the sun
O P
M onstrous but kind
B ouncy and slimy
S leepless and scary
T ough as a boxer
O range as the fruit orange
N ice
E xtraordinary.

Theodore Heapy (6)
Oakthorpe Primary School, Palmers Green

Aron

A mazing world that belongs to me
R eally loves people and monsters because
they are very sweet
O h my goodness, the sun is shining bright
like the light
N o one hates me because I am sweet.

Evelyn Burtea (7)
Oakthorpe Primary School, Palmers Green

Alien

A wesome Awe is as pink as candy,
L ovely, lighthearted bouncy buddy,
I ncredibly spotty, totally dotty,
E normous smile, so sparkly,
N ever nasty, forever friendly.

Anastasia Marcos (6), Zephan, Theo, Aleksandra, Melissa Kotska (7) & Gandom
Oakthorpe Primary School, Palmers Green

Aliens

A brown and scary monster
s L imy as it zooms
I t needs its friends
E ats ice things
N ice monster hides and seeks
S o he has a nice time.

Aman Hussain (7)
Oakthorpe Primary School, Palmers Green

Ugeeb

U geeb hates water
G o and run away from him
E yes like red shining bulbs
E ars like... he has no ears!
B eegu is so scared she will get beaten up!

Haaris Fiyas (7)
Oakthorpe Primary School, Palmers Green

Alien

A s scary as a lost ghost.
L ight purple creature.
I ntelligent, but as cheeky as a monkey.
E nergetic and speedy.
N ice, friendly and kind.

Izabela Toupa (7)

Oakthorpe Primary School, Palmers Green

Unusual Udash

U nthinkable powers and weapons
D ashing jetpack to fly
A lways active for enemies
S cary X-ray vision
H is eyes are white like snow.

Arda Ayyildiz (6)
Oakthorpe Primary School, Palmers Green

Sprony

S illy as a clown
P rickly as a hedgehog
R eally friendly
O nion breath
N ine crazy eyeballs
Y ucky yellow toenails.

Meghan Varnava (7)
Oakthorpe Primary School, Palmers Green

Aliens

A s spotty as chickenpox
L onely as a lost dog
I t is explosive
E ven as green as a leprechaun
N ever be friends with it.

Christina Nicola (7)
Oakthorpe Primary School, Palmers Green

Alien

A s slimy as a slow snail
L ight as a star
I t is a kind, cross monster
E xtremely naughty smile
N ice, ugly octopus.

Eliza Dobrzynska (7)
Oakthorpe Primary School, Palmers Green

Alien

A s fat as a cow
L anding on my world
I t is as annoying as a scream
E normous as a beast
N oisy as a singer.

Marcelo Patrick (7)
Oakthorpe Primary School, Palmers Green

Fluffy

F un and kind
L oves roast chicken
U ses a rocket to fly
F antastic
F riendly
Y ellow and orange.

Mario Paraskeva (6)
Oakthorpe Primary School, Palmers Green

Danish Danger

D rinks blood
A lways angry
N eeds rockets
I s poisonous
S leeps upside down
H orrid but brave.

Danish Ramani (7)
Oakthorpe Primary School, Palmers Green

Aliens

A s pink as a lollipop.
L aunching into space.
I t is explosive.
E xploring the moon.
N ine slithery arms.

Cezary Rzezuchowski (7)
Oakthorpe Primary School, Palmers Green

Emily

E xtraordinarily small.
M unches on fish.
I ncredibly shy.
L ikes to swim.
Y uck! She does not like veg.

Foggy Ford (7)
Oakthorpe Primary School, Palmers Green

Waffle

W hat a cute creature
A squishy, cute alien
F luffy
F riendly
L oves to swim
E ats insects.

Emily Joakim O'Connor (7)
Oakthorpe Primary School, Palmers Green

Eret

E xtraordinarily scary
R eady to make people jump
E ats people like chicken wings
T errifying teeth like scissors.

Keyaan Sooklall (7)
Oakthorpe Primary School, Palmers Green

Alien

A s mighty as a hammer
L aunching into space
I t is explosive
E xploring the moon
N ine slithery arms.

Abdullahi Abdullahi (7)
Oakthorpe Primary School, Palmers Green

Alien

A s slimy as a snail
L aunching into space
I ntelligent
E ver so friendly
N ine slithery arms.

Ziah Leventis (6)
Oakthorpe Primary School, Palmers Green

Glow

G liding through the air
L aughing out loud
O range and red
W ants to scare people.

Jelani Lawal (6)
Oakthorpe Primary School, Palmers Green

Bad, Bad Jet

B ad
A ngry
D isgusting.

J umps
E ats
T eethy.

Muhammad Patel (7)
Oakthorpe Primary School, Palmers Green

Big Boby

B ouncing on a castle
O range like fire
B urning hot
Y ellow like the sun.

Denys Roik (7)
Oakthorpe Primary School, Palmers Green

Evil Jes

J ogging on the green grass
E ats roast chicken
S leeping in the day.

Alexander Velikov (6)
Oakthorpe Primary School, Palmers Green

The Grand National

L oves drinks.
O ne googly eye.
B ottle of monster juice.
acc E ssories that sparkle.
R ound Lober Dober.

D rinks too much.
O pera singer.
B rainless.
E ating cake.
R acing the Grand National.

Aurelia Sowerby (7)
Shocklach Oviatt CE Primary School, Malpas

Rocstar The Monster

R ocstar loves to eat star cookies
O dd, ugly, slimy skin
C ute mouth
S cary monsters
T rouble sometimes, monsters can be trouble
A ngry, Rocstar can get angry
R ocstar is very kind.

Ottilia Chantler (7)
Shocklach Oviatt CE Primary School, Malpas

The Song Of The Monster

S pike is a scared monster.
S **P** ike loves ice cream.
I ce cream is Spike's favourite. "Cake is the best," Spike said.
K ate is in love with Spike
E veryone loves Spike.

Esme MacNaughton (7)

Shocklach Oviatt CE Primary School, Malpas

Zoe's Feelings

Z oe the monster.
O live is her favourite food.
E xciting and enthusiastic whenever
someone is sad to cheer them up.

Dulcie Wood (7)
Shocklach Oviatt CE Primary School, Malpas

Lovely Love Love

L ove is very kind
O ften cheers people on
V ery good at sports
E very day she tells jokes.

Molly Jones (7)
Shocklach Oviatt CE Primary School, Malpas

The Sticky Poem

B ouncing.
L olly.
O range.
B ig blob.
Y oghurt.

Scarlet Burnett (7)
Shocklach Oviatt CE Primary School, Malpas

Blob

B lasts
L oads of
O bstacles
B lech!

Ettolie-Mae Hennigan (7)

Shocklach Oviatt CE Primary School, Malpas

Bob The Monster

B elly button
O ogly legs
B ob likes to run.

Beth Goggins (7)
Shocklach Oviatt CE Primary School, Malpas

Jacklocks

J ack has oozy, green, horrible snot
running down his immensely big nose
A re there eight black legs? Yes, skinny, thin legs
C rammed up heads squished together, one boy, one girl, boy at bottom, girl at top
K icked out of the slow flying tournament, now he's very sad
L ots of pink, shiny eyes looking for ingredients
O h, it's found all of them, now it's cooking for friends
C ooked speedily, they're eating dead cow and sheep
K issing a piece of wood, saying a prayer
S illy dribbling, he's having a second helping.

Bobby Hine (7)

St Nicholas C of E Primary School, Kenilworth

Tickle Monster

T ickle Monster, pink, yellow and blue-
spotted is tickling happily
I t's so fascinating because everything it
does is so straightforwardly
C ome to its house and you get tickled
straightaway!
K iller it is too - its teeth - if you're rude to it
you might not live another day
L ove it with all your heart and you'll get a
nice tickle chase every day!
E veryone for the Tickle Monster, shout
hooray!

M y mum would keep a Tickle Monster as
our pet in the house
O h, sorry to those who like them, it would
eat up every mouse!
N atural it is, but it acts like a human
S oaring in the sky to get away sometimes
T eeth are scary, never use as bait
E veryone thinks it's great!
R oaring it does but it's the best monster
ever!

Seren Thomas (7)

St Nicholas C of E Primary School, Kenilworth

Smokie

S mokie is a good monster but if she smells
baddies she will follow and bite them.
M akes smoke from the top of her head to
make it hard for the baddies to see and
catch her.
O n her sharp, pointy teeth she has
poisonous red and black blood.
K icks baddies and sometimes she kicks
them so hard they get sent away to a far
and distant place.
I nk is the thing she drinks to get smoke
out the chimney on the top of her head.
E ats greedily and sometimes slowly, she
eats all kinds of things and roars. "I am
full!"

Orlagh Dolan (7)
St Nicholas C of E Primary School, Kenilworth

Zompiggy

Z ompiggy has a greeny-yellow body.
O n its head, it has a yellow hard patch and swings its head happily.
M aybe it will watch carefully, looking for its prey.
P eeks as his eyes watch one person with its black, dark eyes.
I t will fight humans nastily with its bloody white arm.
G rabs them and screams loudly before it eats hungrily.
G ets all dirty with its scratchy, giant, dirty dress.
Y ell the prey does in its deep, silver mouth on its round, green, yellow head.

Oliver Williams (7)
St Nicholas C of E Primary School, Kenilworth

Power Belly

P ower Belly's colossal blue body rolls
along the hillside energetically
O n its tiny feet, it stands up carefully
W hen it's scared, it tucks up his feet and
tramples them
E ats greedily at sticky, slimy goo
R ed eyes looking for delicious goo.

B ig mouth eats anything absolutely goo
E nergetically bouncing on bumps
L unges down into a ball, rolls away fast
L urks in the daylight, rolls to goo
Y uck! What a messy monster.

Henry Lough (7)
St Nicholas C of E Primary School, Kenilworth

Crasher

C rasher flies quickly in the pitch-black sky.
R eturning home on planet Mars.
A fter having a warm, cosy bath, he gets downstairs for a warm dinner.
S ometimes he has some ice cream for pudding.
H e has a long, spiky sword and a yellow gun that shoots green, disgusting goo.
E very time before he sleeps, he checks that all of the doors are locked so no one can come in.
R eturning to his bedroom, he checks his alarm so he will wake up. Bedtime!

Him Him Leung (7)
St Nicholas C of E Primary School, Kenilworth

Abbigaille

A bbigaille has long, beautiful, flowing hair.
B ig heart she has because she cares.
B eautiful rainbow body glimmering
I n the night, sometimes she dances enthusiastically.
G iant six colourful tentacles
A nd cute white and black pupils.
I n the flying, starry sea is where she lives.
L arge, pink, slobbery tongue it is.
L ovely, smooth, pink silk wings
E ven when she's in the glimmering blue sea.

Arianna De Maine (7)
St Nicholas C of E Primary School, Kenilworth

Fluffy

F luffy is a kind monster and she has a cute little mouth and she is sleeping majestically. She is
L ooking now, she is moving her mini pink tentacles. She always sleeps
U nder my bed, look, she is sleeping nicely. She is hugging me tightly, I feel so happy that I chose my pet monster, she is so
F luffy! I just forgot, I need to put on her yellow, zigzag crown.
F luffy! Where is she? Phew! She is under the bed!
Y um, yum, it is grass time!

Flora Taylor (6)

St Nicholas C of E Primary School, Kenilworth

Rainbow

R ainbow has jelly friends and it lives in
Rainbow Land
A nd it is kind and polite when eating
rainbow jellyfish in Rainbow Land
I will be your friend if you are nice
N ice to meet people who stick up for
people in danger
B lends in with a big rainbow
O ctopus legs made out of jelly, she uses
them to attack people who are hurting
other people
W hacks people with her antennae, stinging
people who are being mean.

Emilia Tsang (7)
St Nicholas C of E Primary School, Kenilworth

Candyfloss

C andyfloss first on her hoverboard
A prick if you touch her little pink spikes
N ight falls, she's always mysterious
D isco time
Y es, I get a go on her hoverboard
F lying on her hoverboard
L ong, furry, curly hair
O n the hunt for friends to play with
S cratch you if you are not careful
S oft as can be, she's special as she
whizzes past.

Poppy Webb (7)
St Nicholas C of E Primary School, Kenilworth

Crystal Ckrackn

C rystal Ckrackn strongly punches through buildings easily
R apidly he makes thunder and lightning crash down
Y ellow lightning bolts fire across the dark, grey sky
S tomping around with sparkling, green, crystal feet
T ommy drives the colossal, monstrous robot named Crystal Ckrackn
A n ultimate emerald gives Crystal Ckrackn omega power
L ikes green, shiny crystals and emeralds.

Emil Everitt (7)

St Nicholas C of E Primary School, Kenilworth

Levitating Eye

"**L** ead me to the dance party!" he says
E xcellent at spelling
V ery evil
I n valleys he hunts
T ries to find food
A t the park always
T ickle monster
I ts eyeballs are huge
N ut eater
G reat at dancing

E veryone is scared of him
Y ells loudly in ears
E asily wins battles!

Jackson Proctor (7)

St Nicholas C of E Primary School, Kenilworth

Difind

D ifind slowly walks, looking for people.
I n fear, the people hide in caves.
F iner and finer the people grow. They used to be hunters but how the hunter has been hunted.
I n lots of fear, Difind creepily walks into the cave of fear.
N ot one of the people stands up.
D ifind creepily laughs and the people get eaten, the youngest goes, "*Argh!*"

Elwood Robinson (7)
St Nicholas C of E Primary School, Kenilworth

Danger Ranger!

D anger Ranger is always on the lookout
for danger
A nd if she sees danger, she hypnotises you
with her sharp, scanning eyes
N ever go too close to her, she's always
stomping around
G reen, gloopy tongue she has, always
slobbers green, gloopy slime
E yes are dangerous, don't look into them,
she'll hypnotise you
R anger always lies, never trust her!

Bay Bell (7)
St Nicholas C of E Primary School, Kenilworth

Goosking

G lowing tentacles rip and slime, watch out,
it sticks to anything, easy prey, oops!
O ozing hair monster, childish-like
O ffputting face in the puppy dog eyes
S hining bobbles glowing in the distance
K ind, friendly hope in head
I t eats sleepily in the night
N eon heat, it flashes when cold
temperatures
G oing into love mode!

Lucy Wake (7)
St Nicholas C of E Primary School, Kenilworth

Flammer

F iery mane, really mean, do not get seen or die
L ingering fire in his hands, do not get blasted!
A ncient but creeping around in the night
M agnificent tattoos but one is for balance, can you guess?
M ost people died if they came too close!
E asily you can get tricked by him
R oughly playing his games with you, hope you are dreaming.

Rex Griffiths (6)
St Nicholas C of E Primary School, Kenilworth

Raimboa

R aimboa, my monster, has a flame body
and it is very nice
A nd my monster has green eyes that are
shiny
I n my monster house, everything is
rainbow
M y monster has purple teeth
B ig and strong and eats very silly things
O n my monster, he has red, spiky claws
near his arms; my monster is big
A nd strong, it likes being silly.

Edie Watson (7)
St Nicholas C of E Primary School, Kenilworth

Dethkilla

D eathkilla runs in the dead of night
E ating its prey really messily
T eeth bleeding with blood
H orse legs skidding across the floor
K illing everything it sees
I f you touch it, you will be sweltering
L aughing and laughing at you
L ighting its body up with fire
A nd it explodes with angriness.

Jaxon Kenney (7)
St Nicholas C of E Primary School, Kenilworth

Friendly

F luffy is a friendly monster on the hunt for prey.
R ainbow-coloured fur which is super silky.
I can see her lurking around me.
E ating greedily on its prey.
N astily watching.
D igging around for worms to eat.
L eaping around loudly in the trees.
Y uck! Using her small but sharp fangs.

Ophelia Langley (7)
St Nicholas C of E Primary School, Kenilworth

Lollypop

L ollypop Cat
O n the hunt for friends to play with
L eaping up, up, up into the trees
L oving other people when they are hurt
Y ay! It's party time
P ointy, spiky nails for scratching strongly
O ut and about, she creeps sneakily
P icking gold out of the ground, sparkling
brilliantly.

Pippa de Freston-Jones (7)
St Nicholas C of E Primary School, Kenilworth

Fluffy

F luffy is really puffy, his body is full of hair
L ick, lick, slurp, slurp, he drinks his milkshake
U nder the bed he jumps out and scares them all
F luffy is tired, now that night is here he watches the stars and calms down
F luffy wakes up in the morning
Y um yum, his favourite is monster chips.

Federica Liguori (7)
St Nicholas C of E Primary School, Kenilworth

Dangerdude

D rinks gloopy milkshakes.
A lways shows his muscles.
N ever wears shoes.
G reat at spitting gooey slime.
E yes are hypnotising you.
R eally ravishing.
D angerous black eyes.
U nrecognisable, he transforms.
D igs for treasure.
E ighteen years old.

Oscar Woodward (7)
St Nicholas C of E Primary School, Kenilworth

Star

S afe and sound, gleaming in her cave nice
and early, she loves her china teapot. She
is going to have a nice
T ime playing in the green tree park. She
has a meeting
A nd her mummy has signed up to have a
rainbow limo, she is so excited and she
R uns to the park and says, "I think I'm
early..."

Willow Beard (7)
St Nicholas C of E Primary School, Kenilworth

Drippy

D rippy is cool, slime is even better.
R olling the slime to play with it.
I cy and cold because he lives in space.
P olite, thinks when he slurps up stars.
"P erfect," he says, "I want some more."
Y ou can see the food inside of him,
yummy, yum, yum!

Alfie Winter (7)
St Nicholas C of E Primary School, Kenilworth

Sparker

S parker, scary and terrifying.
P owerful his teeth are.
A slimy, gloopy mess he is.
R ed, bulging eyes come out of his head.
K een to pounce out of his cave.
E ats hungrily and messily.
R ed, gloopy slime spreads all over the floor.

Noah Ball (6)
St Nicholas C of E Primary School, Kenilworth

Poizon

P oizon slithers around for delicious food
O h, look out for poisonous fangs!
sl I thering around with a little snake following it
Z apping firebolts from its head, swinging it
O n top of a tree, looking for small food
N uts, he's coming!

James Bury (6)
St Nicholas C of E Primary School, Kenilworth

Slooker

S melly and green.
L ong, flexible fur.
O ne of a kind with a chainsaw-like mouth.
O h no, here it comes! Quick! Run!
K indhearted is not his thing.
E villy and annoyingly he laughs.
R ipping out body parts with red, sharp claws.

Noah Davies (7)
St Nicholas C of E Primary School, Kenilworth

Slippy

S lippy the sea's creature has a kind, innocent smile
L ong, skinny spider arms, I use them to crawl
I like to use my precious core bravely
P icks things up carefully
P eacefully eating some colourful fish
Y eah, I'm very full!

Joseph Bevan (7)
St Nicholas C of E Primary School, Kenilworth

Slimy

S limy is a terrible, nasty, dirty monster
L ike eating spaghetti with it all over his face!
I gnores his bright yellow teeth and eats sweets all day
M assive, sharp, colourful horns that are really bright
Y awn, it's been a bad, bad day.

Georgia Harris (7)
St Nicholas C of E Primary School, Kenilworth

Cutypie

C ute body, white and spotty
U nder deep, dark grass
T wo pointy arms sticking out
Y ou! Are you feeling happy today?
P ointy ears listening carefully
I s it dinnertime yet? It is dinnertime!
E ating, crunching nicely.

Eva Galliana (7)
St Nicholas C of E Primary School, Kenilworth

Feisty

F eisty is a bright blue and pink colour
E ating hungrily and greedily
I t is growling at his prey fiercely
S piky tail is a weapon for people
T eaching students to be smart
Y uck! What a greedy monster.

Olivia Miles (7)
St Nicholas C of E Primary School, Kenilworth

Fluffy

F luffy is a very fluffy ball
L ooks eagerly and rapidly around her
U nder my bed there's Fluffy
F luffy is always happy and nice
F luffy has round, purple eyes
Y ou should not be mean to her.

Amélie Wooldridge (7)
St Nicholas C of E Primary School, Kenilworth

Rocky

R azor-sharp drills, rude to the Eco Council
O h, all of the ores are dropping like flies!
C harging through the rock bank...
Kaboom!
K ick the ores
Y ay! I am the *king of the ores!*

Marshall Symon (7)
St Nicholas C of E Primary School, Kenilworth

Nortey

N aughty, silly nonsense
O n a hunt for silly, funny astronaughties
R are pink pompoms
T he teeth are sparkly white
E ating gracefully and greedily
Y uck! What a messy, greedy monster.

Eloisa Docker (6)
St Nicholas C of E Primary School, Kenilworth

Sily The Monster

S o silly, she can make you laugh all day
I ts long, thin arms tickle you till midnight!
L ong legs with thin arms can scare you up high
Y uck! If you look in her bag there are wet, slobbery eyeballs.

Kimberly Kaleta (7)
St Nicholas C of E Primary School, Kenilworth

Sidney

S idney is a real monster
I t is fluffy and soft
D oes it fly? Nobody knows
N ever make it angry, it's dangerous
E ats meat and likes water
Y ells in the blue clouds.

Henry Bentley (6)
St Nicholas C of E Primary School, Kenilworth

Fluff

F luff can eat cotton candy whenever
L augh your heart out with Fluff!
U p the wakers go with baddies
F luff whacks the bullet place
F luff shoots the bullet and... *kaboom!*

Emma Ashworth (7)
St Nicholas C of E Primary School, Kenilworth

Pom Pom

P om slowly starts to float
O ver it jumps quickly
M oving over the bushes

P om likes bouncing up and down
O n the grass it sleeps
M ind, it's there!

Molly Gilbert (6)
St Nicholas C of E Primary School, Kenilworth

Zomby Head

Z omby Head carries his head.
O h no, he is green so he is a zombie!
M an, I came out of my grave.
B ad Zomby Head, you are too much flying.
Y ucky, dusty trousers.

Archie Rose (6)
St Nicholas C of E Primary School, Kenilworth

Terry

T erry is a rainbow monstrous monster
E ats viciously and hungrily
R unning rapidly across the roads
R acing loudly versus Lamborghini
Y eah, it's good!

Harry Slade (6)

St Nicholas C of E Primary School, Kenilworth

Slima

S lima, slimy and gooey, he
L ooks for prey
I s it yummy? Yes, it is, eating
M essily, watch him eat more
A nd with eating, "Argh! I am sick!"

William Sale (6)
St Nicholas C of E Primary School, Kenilworth

Bigun

B igun has purple, stinky socks.
I ts green, floppy arms sticking out.
G reen, fat body out.
U nder his legs are puddles.
k N obbly knees are shaking.

Eliza O'Halloran (7)
St Nicholas C of E Primary School, Kenilworth

Sharpy

S harpy eats ferociously
H ow he plans secretly
A fter he moves dramatically
R uns revoltingly
P owerfully lands
Y ep, that's him!

Alexander Ruffle (7)
St Nicholas C of E Primary School, Kenilworth

Fuzzle

F unny Fuzzle with scary teeth
U nusual
Z ooms quickly, has spikes
Z ooms quickly, trail of slime
L aser
E very day lots of sleep.

Caiden Baker (6)

St Nicholas C of E Primary School, Kenilworth

Toxic

T racks people from afar
O n the first head, it has slimy teeth
X -ray vision and laser eyes
I t has two big heads
C atches prey very fast.

Odysseas Karapapas-Fiamegkos (6)
St Nicholas C of E Primary School, Kenilworth

Monster

M unching on worms
O range, pink and blue
N ose so long
S ticky hands
T errible smell
E yes so small
R uns quickly.

Peppy Kay (7)
St Nicholas C of E Primary School, Kenilworth

Mankee

M ankee is serious
A lways eating children
N ever moves quickly
K nocking knees
E ye like a ball
E veryone loves him.

George (6)
St Nicholas C of E Primary School, Kenilworth

Lola

L ovely and kindhearted to other monsters.
O h, a flower, yes, please! Soft fur.
L ittle, goes up and down.
A cute eye with a heart in it.

Aria Wright (7)
St Nicholas C of E Primary School, Kenilworth

Wary

W arm, fluffy, blue fur
A big mouth with green teeth
R unning quickly on grass
Y ucky pink tongue.

Cobi Rowley (7)
St Nicholas C of E Primary School, Kenilworth

Theo

T akes other people's food
H e eats hungrily
E ats loudly
O ne big eye.

Theo Thomas (7)
St Nicholas C of E Primary School, Kenilworth

Impeccable

I n my most comforting life moment is sharing
M emories with the ones I love, like treasures
P erfectly crafted to showcase the heart beating
E xcitement of joy, melting away, time stopping
C apacities of wonders that illuminate
C ontagious heartaches that laughter can cure
A mplifying Mom and Dad's laughter as they
B elieve, play and dance with me, creating memories
L asting forever like the sea and sand colliding together
E very time that is spent with me is a treasure in my eye, kids love attention too.

Goodness Oyeleye (5)
St Peter's CE Primary School, Chorley

Funnychops!

F unny, fishy jokes
U mbrella for a hat
N ice and loved
N ever sleeps at bedtime
Y o-yo tricks to make you laugh
C at ears and swishy tail
H ungry all the time
O range fluffy fur
P retty love heart eyes
S illiest monster in the world!

Emily Chetwynd (5)
St Peter's CE Primary School, Chorley

Friendly

F riendly is cuddly and fluffy
R eally funny character
I think he might be a bit smelly
E very day he will grant you a wish
N ow he has a big eye
D ay before yesterday he won a race
L ife in the sun
Y ay! He loves flowers.

Lila Stoneman (5)
St Peter's CE Primary School, Chorley

Stiggy

S tiggy is a monster who is very big and strong
T wig-like to camouflage and jump off the trees
I s very friendly and very long
G reen leaves for his hair
G rabs any litter that he sees on the floor
Y ou wouldn't spot him in the woods.

Fred Kilpatrick-Ivers (5)
St Peter's CE Primary School, Chorley

Monster Train

T rain full of monsters
R apidly travelling along the rails to
Monster Land
A ll of a sudden, the whistle is blown to
stop the train
I n the darkness, bats fly past with glowing
red eyes
N ow time to alight the train and head to
Monster Land!

William Robert McGurk (7)
St Peter's CE Primary School, Chorley

The Glow

G low in the dark monster
L ights up the night
O nly to be seen
W hen I turn out the light
I n the corner standing
N ice and still
G lorious glow expanding, my room it fills!

Eliza Sharples (6)
St Peter's CE Primary School, Chorley

Colourful

C old monster
O nly friendly
L ots of good friends
O range body
U ses a wand
R ainbow claws
F inds gold
U nder the clouds
L oves to jump.

Chloe Yung (6)
St Peter's CE Primary School, Chorley

Maisie

M y monster loves me
A ll morning my monster makes breakfast
I t comes and gives me cuddles
S he likes to play
I t looks after me
E very day it makes me smile.

Olivia Hutchinson (7)
St Peter's CE Primary School, Chorley

Crunch

C olourful fire
R eaches two mountains
U ses its claws for scratching
N otice the spikes on its back like a samurai
C runches bones
H e has sharp teeth.

Archie Edwards (6)
St Peter's CE Primary School, Chorley

Rainbow

R ainbow the monster
A lways eats cheese
I s sometimes scary
N o one hides
B est of friends
O ut of this world
W onderfully funny.

Grace Birnie (7)
St Peter's CE Primary School, Chorley

Squodge

S leeps in a cave
Q uite scary
U gly eyes
O range, disgusting fingers
D rippy mouth
G rabs goats to eat
E ats anything.

Leo Campkin (5)
St Peter's CE Primary School, Chorley

Jack

J ack has two purple eyes
A ll he wants to do is draw
C ute he is with a crown
K ing Jack is pink and hairy.

Maya Kogut (4)
St Peter's CE Primary School, Chorley

Necla

N eighbourhood monster
E ight eyes
C reamy and creepy skin
L ovely monster
A mazing smile.

Himanya Hrulthasan (7)
St Peter's CE Primary School, Chorley

Heat

H e is huge.
E yes are powerful.
A pair of purple ripped shorts.
T he ends of the horns are sharp.

Rupert Green (6)
St Peter's CE Primary School, Chorley

Jboy

J oyful at all times
B eautifully created
O bedience is key
Y es! You are it, yes! You can do it!

Oroolorun Olayiwola (5)
St Peter's CE Primary School, Chorley

Bouncer

B ounces up and down
O ne hat on his head
U ses a bouncer because he has no legs
N ice and colourful
C leverly kicks a football when he sees one
E ats slime burgers
R eally has a big smile.

Everly Harrison (6)
Truro School Prep, Highertown

Fireball

F ire skin.
I s slimy and poisonous.
R uns really fast.
E ats smoothies every day.
B lue claws.
A lways poisonous.
L oves to shoot fire.
L ives deep underground.

Atticus Ducker-Cobb (5)
Truro School Prep, Highertown

Hillgarn

H orns like a bull
I t has fangs
L ives in the snow
L oves to eat meat
G iant wings
A lways hunts
R uns slowly
N octurnal.

Otis Barclay (5)
Truro School Prep, Highertown

Mellow

M y monster is called Mellow
E ats honey every day
L earns new things every day
L istens very well
O wns a lot of things
W ears lots of colours.

Eleanor Viqueira (5)
Truro School Prep, Highertown

Laser

L ong, scary, dangerous body
A club at the end of his tail
S cary head
E ats lots of chocolate
R eally good at climbing.

Will Gardner (6)
Truro School Prep, Highertown

Creeper

C reepy eyes
R uns at night
E ats pigs
E njoys oats
P lease stay away
E normous body
R uns slow.

Hugo Cudworth (5)
Truro School Prep, Highertown

Snoopy

S noopy is
N aughty, he has an
O range tail
O ften jumps up and down
P urple legs
Y ellow face.

Pippa Vernon (5)
Truro School Prep, Highertown

Spotty

S potty loves you!
P lays and
O ften he sleeps and he loves
T ickles
T oo much. He
Y aps.

Arabella Coninck Farr (6)
Truro School Prep, Highertown

Arrowy

A ngry Arrowy
R ed face
R uns fast
O ften eats meat
W ears spikes
Y ucky slobber.

Edith Hougham (6)
Truro School Prep, Highertown

Toxic

T eeth that are shiny
O range googly eyes
X -ray vision
I t fights
C old monster.

Theo Ryan (6)
Truro School Prep, Highertown

Nessy

N essy
E ats nectar and
S leeps in a nest, it is
S cary with three
Y ellow beaks.

Bethany Day (6)
Truro School Prep, Highertown

Stripy

S tormy character
T iny eyes
R eally scary and
I s
P esky and
Y ucky.

Ernie Alken (6)
Truro School Prep, Highertown

Slimy

S tinky monster
L ikes to eat slime
I t smells bad
M akes slime
Y ellow fur.

Albee King (5)
Truro School Prep, Highertown

Mr Eye

M ighty arms
R uns away from...

E lephants
Y ellow slime and
E rnie.

Theo Hendy (5)
Truro School Prep, Highertown

Fang

F angs are poisonous
A ngry and spiky
N aughty and nasty
G reen fangs are deadly.

Henry Richards (5)

Truro School Prep, Highertown

Fluffy

F lappy Fluffy
L ikes
U gly
F angs and
F inds
Y ummy food.

Evie Simpson (5)
Truro School Prep, Highertown

Jelly

J iggly arms
E ats cake
L oves flowers
L ikes slime
Y ucky fingers.

Clemmie Chrusciak (6)
Truro School Prep, Highertown

George

G iant George
E ats meat
O nly
R aw and
G ulps
E ggs.

William Christie (6)
Truro School Prep, Highertown

Minty

M inty
I s
N aughty and incredibly
T ough. Also loud and
Y appy.

Althea Welch (6)
Truro School Prep, Highertown

Honey

H as horns and
O range fur
N ice
E yes and
Y ellow tongue.

Catherine Lambert (6)
Truro School Prep, Highertown

Minty

M ighty Minty
I s
N ice and
T ries
Y ummy food.

Austin Pietroni (6)
Truro School Prep, Highertown

Cutie

C lever monster
U ses
T alons
I n
E verything.

Ted Long (5)
Truro School Prep, Highertown

Spidermon

S pidermon has soft skin
P opcorn is his favourite food
I s very fluffy
D oesn't like broccoli
E verybody wants to hug Spidermon
R emember not to mess with him
M onday is his least favourite day of the week
O n a sunny day, he likes to walk on the beach
N ever make him angry.

Freddie Press (5)
Westerton Primary Academy, Tingley

Burple The Purple Friendly Monster

B urple the purple monster is a smiley,
happy monster.
U sually, he spends all his time with his
friends.
R eally he's quite handsome.
P urple is his favourite colour, just like his
silky skin.
L illy, his friend, plays with him because
he's kind.
E verybody wants to be friends with Burple!

Bobby Rigby (6)
Westerton Primary Academy, Tingley

The Poem Of Slimy Bob

S limy Bob is friendly.
L ies a lot.
I have to tell him off.
M y sister thinks he's funny.
Y ou'll see what he's like.

B ut he always listens to how I feel
O n days that I feel sad.
B ob is the best friend I could ever have!

Oliver Green (6)
Westerton Primary Academy, Tingley

Violet

V iolet is a very happy monster
I ndigo is Violet's shy, black cat
O bstacle courses are one of her hobbies
L ives in a castle in Monster Town
E ating chewing gum and blowing bubbles
T ries to make friends every day.

Emily Wilson (6)
Westerton Primary Academy, Tingley

Devilish

D evilish is my monster
E vil most days
V ery deadly
I n lots of ways
L ikes to tell lies
I s most unfriendly
S o keep away when he's in a
H orrid, devilish frenzy!

Jaxon Watts (5)
Westerton Primary Academy, Tingley

Smuggley Monster

S muggley is my monster
M ean as can be
U gly and smelly
G reen as a tree
G iant and grizzly
L ots of sharp teeth
E yes, he has eight
Y ikes! Don't catch me.

Avah Barstow (5)
Westerton Primary Academy, Tingley

Biggles

B iggles is his name
I n the big monster world
G reen tongue
G reen slugs he eats
L oves catching flies with his long tongue
E njoys playing with friends
S hiny skin.

Maddie Bishop-West (6)
Westerton Primary Academy, Tingley

Squelchy

S limy as can be
Q uite fast
U h-oh, he ate my paper
E verybody likes him
L oves slime
C an jump really high
H as lots of friends
Y ou can be his friend.

Dylan Lister (6)
Westerton Primary Academy, Tingley

Scaley

S limy scales like a snake.
C reepy eyes.
A lways eats children who are naughty.
L ong legs to run fast.
E vil eyes to see everything.
Y ellow body to shine bright.

Alicia Raud (5)
Westerton Primary Academy, Tingley

One Eye Bluebell

B luebell the monster
L oves to eat slime
U nder his rock
E njoys telly
B oings around
E ating garbage
L icking moss
L ong legs.

Mason Dalby (5)
Westerton Primary Academy, Tingley

Henry's Yellow Monster

Y ellow has yellow skin
E xcited for the final
L oves to eat soup and slime
L ate to school
O n school holidays he goes on a holiday
W alks slowly.

Henry Lumley (6)

Westerton Primary Academy, Tingley

Stars The Scorpion

S tars is a scorpion.
T oday Stars ate rubbish out of the bins.
A fter dinner, he played at the park.
R eady with his pinching claws.
S tars played Minecraft.

Dominic Pilkington (6)
Westerton Primary Academy, Tingley

Indigo

I n the night, I
N ever make friends
D on't come near me at all
I t is my house
G o away, you stinky monsters
O nly purple monsters allowed.

Sophie Hedderick (5)
Westerton Primary Academy, Tingley

Pikachu Is The Best

P ikachu is the best
I love him the most
K eep trying to win
A ll the badges
C atch them all
H ow good are you?
U nstoppable.

Jude Greenwood (5)
Westerton Primary Academy, Tingley

Blobby The Monster

B lobby the monster is hairy
L ooks like a mammoth
O r like a whale
B ut he is friendly
B ecause he goes to school
Y es, we all love him!

Grace Overend (5)
Westerton Primary Academy, Tingley

Slosley

S oft
L oves hugs
O atmeal is his favourite meal
S cary monster face
L ovely smile
E normous eyes
Y ellow teeth.

Eleonora Boeva (6)
Westerton Primary Academy, Tingley

Stinky

S melly monster
T ook a bath
I n a muddy puddle
N ow he's stinky and dirty
K ing of the mud
Y ellow fur is now brown.

Amelie Roadnight (6)
Westerton Primary Academy, Tingley

Terror Of Flames

F lies around on a surfboard
L oves fires
A lways a million degrees
M ainly eats flamy fish
E ven drinks lava
S mall.

Sebastian Plauborg Varley (6)
Westerton Primary Academy, Tingley

Stinky

S mells really bad
T alks really strange
I s really friendly
N ot really scary
K een to eat worms
Y ucky, yuck, yuck!

Sonny Trenam-Yates (6)
Westerton Primary Academy, Tingley

Blobs The Funny Monster

B lack monster
L oves to play games
"O uch!" he shouted
"B lobs is my name
S omeone stepped on my foot!"

Irhaa Khan (6)
Westerton Primary Academy, Tingley

Monster Friend

M ary made a friend that is you.
A nd her yellow head is glowing.
R ed body is shining bright.
Y o-yoing is her favourite thing to do.

Isobel Gloria Bowker (5)
Westerton Primary Academy, Tingley

Fluffy

F unny little monster
L ikes to play
U nder my bed
F riendly little monster
F luffy and silly
Y ellow and red.

Mila-Maria Rimkeviciute (6)
Westerton Primary Academy, Tingley

Danny

D anny loves football
A pples are his favourite fruit
N ever eats people
N ice and cuddly
Y ellow fur everywhere.

Orla Norton (6)
Westerton Primary Academy, Tingley

C-3po

C aring is my monster
3 times he likes to twirl
P ut a smile upon your face
O r my monster will turn into a fairy.

Sophie O'Donnell (5)
Westerton Primary Academy, Tingley

My Best Friend Stitch

S oft and cuddly
T iny teeth
I ncredibly happy
T errific friend
C ute smile
H olds my hand.

Lauren Maloney (6)
Westerton Primary Academy, Tingley

Klaus

K laus the monster
L oves to play ball
A big eyeball
U ses his tongue to smell
S ees in infrared.

Aaron Wilson
Westerton Primary Academy, Tingley

Posh

P osh the monster
O lives are her favourite food
S hopping at Claire's Accessories
H appy little monster.

Agnes Skitt (5)

Westerton Primary Academy, Tingley

Circly

C ool and calm
I ntelligent
R eally friendly
C heeky
L oving
Y oghurt maker, yum yum!

Mia Phull (6)

Westerton Primary Academy, Tingley

Spot

S pot the ladybird
P lays with Dot the ant
O ver in the park, they play chase
T hey play all night and day.

Pearl Jamu (6)
Westerton Primary Academy, Tingley

Silly Lily

S melly feet
I nteresting facts
L ovely spikes
L ucky all the time
Y ou will love her.

Lori Wright (6)
Westerton Primary Academy, Tingley

Roz

R oz the head monster
O ccasionally loves to write
Z igzagging through the students while she reads a book.

Jackson Preston (5)

Westerton Primary Academy, Tingley

Slimy

S limy slug
L oves bubbles
I ce cream is the best
M onster fun
Y ummy mud.

Ellie Sampson (6)
Westerton Primary Academy, Tingley

Slosh

S losh the monster
L ots of legs
O ne big eye
S mart
H e has wings.

Ernie Morley (6)
Westerton Primary Academy, Tingley

YoungWriters Est. 1991

Young Writers Information

We hope you have enjoyed reading this book – and that you will continue to in the coming years.

If you're the parent or family member of an enthusiastic poet or story writer, do visit our website **www.youngwriters.co.uk/subscribe** and sign up to receive news, competitions, writing challenges and tips, activities and much, much more! There's lots to keep budding writers motivated!

If you would like to order further copies of this book, or any of our other titles, then please give us a call or order via your online account.

Young Writers
Remus House
Coltsfoot Drive
Peterborough
PE2 9BF
(01733) 890066
info@youngwriters.co.uk

Join in the conversation!
Tips, news, giveaways and much more!

YoungWritersUK   YoungWritersCW   youngwriterscw

Scan me to watch the
Monster Acrostics Video